101+ Creative Journaling Prompts

Inspiration for Journaling and an
Introduction to Art Journaling

Peddler Arts
Publishing & Design

101+ Creative Journaling Prompts
Inspiration for Journaling and
an Introduction to Art Journaling

First Edition

Copyright © 2012 by Kristal Norton
All rights reserved.
ISBN-10: 0692614605
ISBN-13: 978-0692614600

Designer: Peddler Arts
Artwork: Kristal Norton

Printing/manufacturing information for this book may be found on the last page.

Table of Contents

Introduction

Journaling is an amazing tool to help you work through emotions, to document the special moments in life, and to express yourself. But whether you are new to journaling, or have been at it for years, I'm sure you've had days where you simply don't know what to write about. I've come across this problem one too many times myself... so I've brainstormed, researched, and compiled 101 of my most favorite, inspiring prompts to refer to when I'm stuck.

Sometimes I answer a prompt directly, and other times just reading them sparks something else inside of me. They have helped me to get to know myself better, get thinking, and have inspired me. So, I'm sharing my personal list of prompts with you in hopes that they will serve you as well as they have been serving me.

But these prompts are not only great for traditional journaling; they're inspiring for art journaling as well. As an avid art journaler, I have found these prompts to be a great starting point for many of my most favorite art journal pages. Throughout this book, I share images of my art journal pages inspired by the prompts, in hopes that they show you how each prompt can be used and interpreted in many ways.

As a bonus, I have for you an exclusive private video of me choosing a random prompt from the book and creating an art journal page from start to finish. I hope it gives you a better idea of how a prompt can inspire a whole art journal page instead of just giving you a starting point for traditional journaling. (A link to the private video is included in the Bonus section.)

If art journaling has you intrigued, I've also included 20 of my favorite art prompts to help get you loosened up. They are so quick and easy that even a beginner would enjoy. I hope they inspire you to start a creative journal if you've never tried it before. If you do art journal, may they be an inspiration for you when you're feeling stuck.

May you never be at a loss for inspiration again!

The Magic of Art Journaling

While journaling alone can help free yourself of mental burdens and allow you to live your life in awareness; when paired with creativity... it creates even more magic.

But don't be scared off by the words "creativity" or "art". Anyone can art journal, even if you can't draw a stick figure! Art journaling is simply the act of combining imagery with words in order to express yourself. Even the word "imagery" can be taken loosely. Just start with whatever you feel comfortable with, whether it be scribbles, doodling, photos, or magazine clippings. There are no rules in art journaling; it's all about experimenting, play-ing, and discovering your true self.

When you start to express yourself visually along with your words, your creative spirit begins to soar free. (And yes, even you too have a creative spirit!) You release and express more of your emotions, and you dig deeper into who you are as a person. The simple act of adding color, scribbles, or im-agery to your journal will cause you to spill open more and create with such freedom that it allows you to find the clarity and self awareness you didn't even know you were searching for.

To learn more about creative journaling, visit my blog for a free Art Journaling 101 e-Course. This isn't your average art journaling course where I as the artist try to teach you how to use paint and other mediums like I do... oh no. I understand that art journaling is a personal experience, where each person develops their own style and preferences. Within the free e-course, I touch upon supplies and techniques you may want to try, but we focus more on finding time to journal, overcoming fears, finding your style, and more through videos, articles, and images. Come on over and experience the world of art journaling.

You can register for the free class at: http://kristalnorton.com/art-journaling-101/

Using This Book

When at a loss for words, you can simply flip through the book until one of the prompts "speaks" to you. Instead of going through the book from beginning to end, use it as a reference to find a prompt that inspires you in the moment.

If you'd rather be surprised and are up for a challenge, you can choose a prompt randomly. I have provided (in the Bonus section) a link to download a PDF version of all the prompts in this book. Simply print it out, cut the prompts out into individual strips, and then keep them in a pretty container on your desk. That way, they will be right at your fingertips when you need them most, and you can pluck one from the container for an instant challenge.

Hopes, Dreams, & Goals

What is something you want to learn how to do?

What is something you wish you could know about?

What's your wildest dream?

What is something that you are always wishing for?

What would you do if money were no object?

What is something you wish you could do?

What is something you want to do better than you do now?

What would your perfect day look like?

What did you do this week that brought you closer
to your goals?

List 25 fun things you'd like to do this summer.

What would you do if you know you couldn't fail?

Write out a bucket list, i.e., things you want to do or accomplish before you pass.

What place do you wish you could visit right now?

(Below is an example of an art journal page I created using the previous prompt.)

Life's Moments

Tell about something that is beautiful to you.

If you could relive one moment from yesterday what would it be? Describe it in detail.

What is the best thing that ever happened to you?

Tell about something that made you want to do better.

How did you wear your hair as a child? Did you like it or hate it? Is there a specific memory that comes to mind?

Tell about something that made you feel thankful.

Describe a childhood memory that you would love to relive.

Write about a memory involving food, e.g., did your grandmother make a special treat on holidays?

Tell about something that taught you an important lesson.

What is the best advice you've ever received?

What was your favorite toy as a child? Describe the toy, or write about a memory involving it.

Describe an accomplishment that you are most proud of.

What is the biggest mistake you made this week?

Journal about an imaginary friend you had as a child. What did you do together? How did people react? If you've never had one... make one up now.

What is something you wish you could do over?

What is your very first memory?

What was your favorite band growing up? Do you remember any of your favorite song lyrics?

What's the stupidest thing you've ever done?

As a child, who was your favorite relative and why?

(Below is an example of an art journal page I created using the previous prompt.)

Being You

What is something that you could teach someone else how to do?

Are you superstitious? What are you superstitious about?

What is something wonderful that makes you different from everyone else?

What is your favorite thing to wear? Why?

What is something that you know is true?

What scares you?

What are some song lyrics that mean something to you?

What are the freedoms that you appreciate and why?

List a few professions that you wanted to be when you were young. What regrets or thankfulness do you feel about not pursuing each of these professions?

What is the most important thing you do every
day?

What is something you feel really proud of?

How do you indulge yourself? Do you need to indulge yourself more often?

What holds you back?

What is something that makes you really happy?

What is your favorite treat?

What things do you appreciate today?

Who would you trust your deepest secrets to? If no one, then why?

What makes you feel vulnerable?

Make a list of 10 people you are thankful for being in your life.

Write out your favorite quote.

What is your biggest fear?

What motivates you to take action?

List or journal about all the things you love in life.

(Below is an example of an art journal page I created using the previous prompt.)

Personal Growth

What is something you have learned about friend-
ship?

Write a letter to your younger self. What would you like him/her to know to prepare for his/her future?

Write a letter that you could have received from yourself ten years from now. What would your future self have to tell you?

What is something you have learned in a book?

What character traits do you need to work on?

If you could change one thing about your life to make it better, what would it be?

What is something you have learned about being kind?

What are your biggest values? How can you portray
them more in your daily life?

Was there a specific event in your life that inspired you to be a better person?

What is something you have learned about telling the truth?

Write your obituary as if you died yesterday. How would it look twenty years from now?

What is something you have learned about family?

Write about five different ways you can become a
better person.

Tell a story about when you were a beginner (at anything). How far have you come since then?

What have you always been curious about?

(Below is an example of an art journal page I created using the previous prompt.)

Storytelling

What would you change if you were in charge of the world?

Do you believe there is life on other planets? Why?

What other point in time do you think you would fare well in? How would your life be different?

What does the word 'miracle' mean to you?

Close your eyes and imagine the kind of world you would like to see. What is it like?

If you could be anyone else (fictional or non) for a day, who would it be and why?

Make a list of 25 words or phrases that come to mind when you think of Halloween (or other holiday)

What would you do if you found yourself suddenly rich?

If you had a super power, what would it be? List ten good things and ten bad things you would do with it.

Rip out an image from a magazine and glue it into this page. Then, make up a story about the person or objects in the photo.

If you could become a member of any TV family, which would it be and why?

Do you own an object of great value to you even though it isn't worth a lot of money? Write about what it is and why it's important to you.

What would you do if you could live a day without consequences?

What was one of your biggest failures in which you learned a valuable lesson?

If you could make it rain anything besides water, what would it be? (E.g. gummy bears, leaves, beer) What would be the effect?

(Below is an example of an art journal page I created using the previous prompt.)

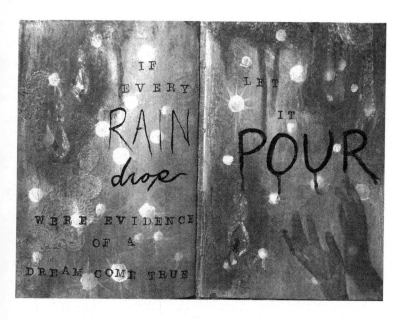

Finish the Sentence

Life is...

One thing I want to accomplish this month is...

Nobody knows that I...

My favorite place to go is...

When I'm happy...

The smell of cake makes me think of...

I feel _____ years old inside because...

If I had no work or other obligations tomorrow, I would...

I used to think...

Before my time ends...

I wish I was...

I remember when...

3am feels like...

The greatest gift I've ever been given...

I wonder...

I am proud of myself for...

I am grateful for...

I would never...

I believe...

(Below is an example of an art journal page I
created using the previous prompt.)

Art Prompts

Adding color or visuals to your journal can add not only interest, but another layer of meaning. Try playing with these prompts to explore visual journaling.

* Doodle a "list" of twenty or more things that describe you. For example, if you love photography, you could doodle a camera. If you have curly hair, you could doodle some curls.

* Find papers around the house to collage in your journal, such as gift tissue paper, phone book pages, receipts, etc.

* Cut out an image (or partial image) from a magazine, glue into your journal then doodle around it to make a new image. For example, perhaps you find an image of a toaster... you could then doodle around it, using the toaster as a head for a robot.

* Squirt some acrylic paint onto your page. Move it around with an old credit card or key card. Scrape the paint up and down, and then scrape side to side, letting the colors mix slightly.

* Choose a color, then fill your page with anything and everything that is that color. You can try to find magazine images or wrapping paper in your chosen color, or look around at other things in your home such as yarn, string, things in your junk drawer, fabric scraps, gift tags, stickers, etc.

* If you are a coffee or tea drinker, try splashing a few drops onto your journal page. When dry, imagine what these splotches look like, kind of like looking up at the clouds, and then sketch in some details.

* Dip a string or yarn into paint. Place it in your journal, and then shut the book leaving the end hanging out. While the book is still closed, pull the string out.

* Experiment with stamping patterns using paint and items found around your home or yard such as leaves, potatoes, toilet paper tube, etc.

* Paint your page with watercolor. While the paint is still wet, sprinkle with table salt and watch the magic happen as it dries! (When completely dry, you can brush away the salt.)

* Create a really ugly drawing.

* Glue down a page from an old book into your journal. Highlight or circle words that call to you, or highlight words to create a new sentence. Paint or color with a marker around your words to block out the rest.

* Using letters cut out from a magazine, spell out your favorite quote.

* Put your journal or piece of paper somewhere outside so that a shadow casts on it (such as a shadow of a flower). Sketch the shadow.

* Flip to the second empty page in your art journal. Draw one or more doors, and then use an exacto knife to cut one side so that you can open the door(s). Glue the opposing pages together (just don't glue the door(s) shut!), then write down secrets or hidden surprises within the doors.

* Fill the page with circles.

* Grab a pack of crayons or other art supplies from your child's stash and play like you were five again.

* Tear out sections of color and texture from a magazine or scraps of art. "Sculpt" them into a scene on your page.

* Using one or more writing utensils of your choice (E.g. pencil, pen, markers, crayons), draw parallel lines with each line being different. You can draw thick lines, thin lines, curly lines, jagged lines, etc. Keep going until you fill the page.

* Fill the entire page with mindless doodles.

* Choose one word that describes what you are feeling today. Write that word again and again all over your page until it is completely filled up. Be creative! Use different colors, fonts, styles, or perhaps even use letters found in a magazine.

(Below is an example of an art journal page I created using this last prompt.)

Bonus Material

As a gift for purchasing this book, I have for you a bonus video of me creating an art journal page from start to finish. I hope it gives you an idea of how a prompt can inspire a whole art journal page instead of just giving you a starting point for traditional journaling.

I also offer a PDF version of all the prompts in this book so that you can print, cut out, and put them in a jar for easy access when you're feeling stuck.

Access your bonus material at:

http://kristalnorton.com/101-creative-journaling-prompts-bonus-material/

About the Author

Kristal Norton is a wife, mother, creative explorer, and mixed media artist living by the sea in Connecticut.

Her days are led by the belief that taking the time for creative play and to listen to our soul is essential to living a fulfilling life.

In her role as a creative life coach, Kristal seeks to help others reclaim and celebrate their innate brilliance through the use of creativity - a hidden power we ALL possess.

Learn more about Kristal and her adventures in art journaling and creative soul expression, as she shares her musings on cultivating the authentic self via inspirational e-books, videos, and articles on her website and blog at KristalNorton.com

Made in the USA
Lexington, KY
14 July 2017